# Chicken Nugget Love

## A True Story Of
## A Boy & His Love For Chicken Nuggets

Written By:

Steven M Roper

Illustrated by:

Thakshi dissanayake

First, I would like to thank the most high. Secondly, my amazing family. Without you guys I wouldn't be strong enough to endure adversity and overcome all of the daily challenges. My kids, thank you for pushing daddy to be all he can be every single day.

I'd like to show much appreciation to everyone who's ever seen something in me and told me to never give up. Even more appreciation to anyone who's ever taught me something or coached me. All of the unplanned mentorship I received has been a true blessing.

I love learning, I love being creative, and I love putting smiles on other peoples faces. I really hope you enjoy this short story.
**Thank you!**

*"If I am the wisest man alive, it is for I know one thing, and that is that I know nothing."- Socrates*

I would like to dedicate this
to my son King Maurice Roper.
Sorry for the entire year of 2022
and I promise I'm gone spend
the rest of my life making
it up to you.
**I love you son!**

There once was a boy named King who loved his chicken nuggets more than anything.

**King loved them when he played.**
**King loved them when he cleaned.**

King loved them when he cried and he loved them when he would sing.

King loved them in the day and he loved them late at night.

King could take his time or he could eat them in one bite.

King's love for chicken nuggets
was really hard to explain.

King's parents couldn't break it, but they knew something had to change.

Juicy or crispy, dinosaur shaped or perfectly round.

King wanted his chicken nuggets and he wanted them right now.

King didn't care if they was fresh out the over or if they had set around.

King was so in love with chicken nuggets that he couldn't put them down.

His mom would offer him healthier foods like meatloaf, fish, and lasagna.

And King would say, "No, can we get chicken nuggets from McDonald's? "

His dad would offer him snack foods like burgers, pizza, and tacos.

King parents had enough of this chicken nugget love.

They sat King down and explained it was time to eat some different stuff.

At first he whined and fussed,
but they wasn't letting up.

That night he left and stayed with his friend Dinero.

And came back home with a love
for cereal.

# The End

CPSIA information can be obtained
at www.ICGtesting.com
Printed in the USA
JSHW041446100922
30288JS00012B/236